THE
HOUSEPLANTS
COLORING BOOK

THE
HOUSEPLANTS
COLORING BOOK

Maria Lia
Malandrino

SIRIUS

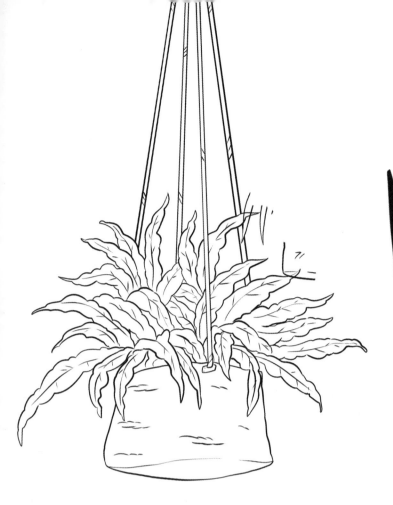

SIRIUS

This edition published in 2023 by Sirius Publishing, a division of
Arcturus Publishing Limited,
26/27 Bickels Yard, 151–153 Bermondsey Street,
London SE1 3HA

Copyright © Arcturus Holdings Limited

ISBN: 978-1-3988-3022-6
CH011173NT
Supplier 29, Date 1023, Print run 00004211

Printed in China

Introduction

No home is really complete without a plant or two to add to its décor. Whether you choose plants for interesting foliage or to add color, there is something uplifting about bringing a bit of nature indoors.

Some exotic plants obviously need lots of care and attention, but many others are far hardier and easier to maintain, such as ivies, ferns, succulents, and cacti. All you need to do is establish a watering regime that works and find the right position in terms of sunlight that the plant prefers.

The images in *The Houseplants Coloring Book* celebrate a wide variety of plants and flowers that are often found in homes around the world, including spring-flowering bulbs, like hyacinths and narcissi, delicate-blooming miniature roses, vibrant hibiscus, and jungle-like palms. And, just as plants can induce a sense of calm, so can spending a peaceful half hour or more as you sit down with a set of colored pens or pencils and select one of the delightful images in this book to bring to life.

So, enjoy your coloring and immerse yourself in the wonderful images that have been specially created for this collection.

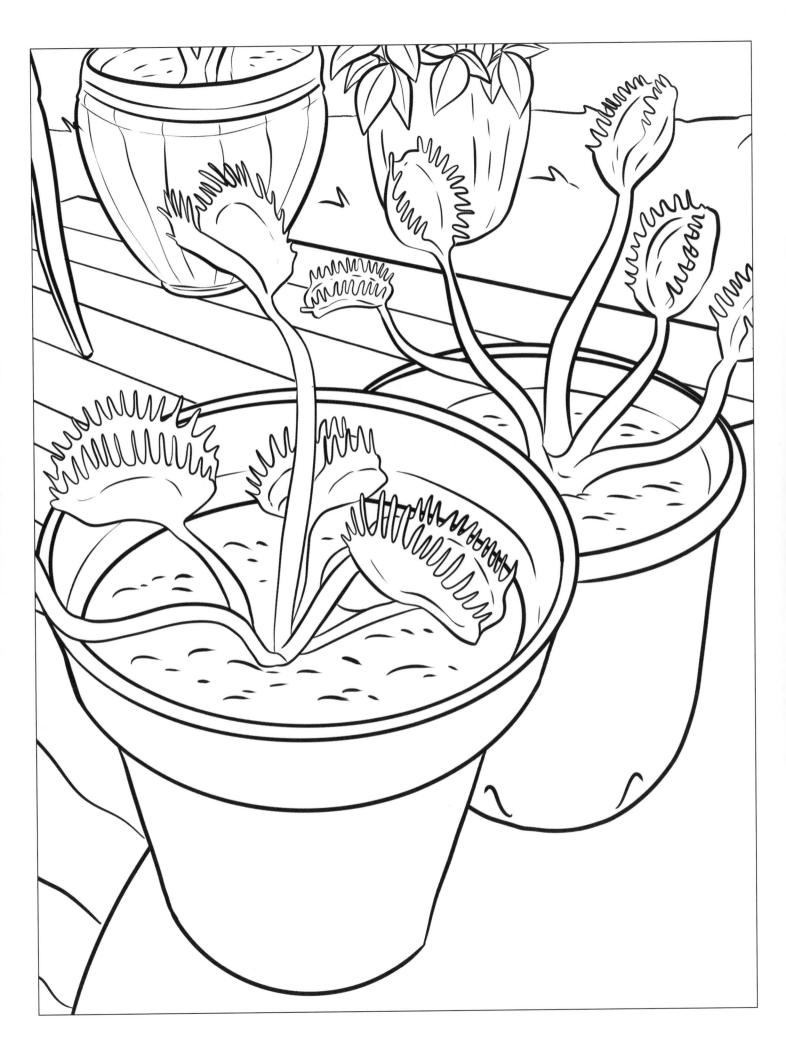

Index of Plants